THE THREE PENNY BANKS

REINALDO DOMINGOS

dsop editora

AUTHOR
REINALDO DOMINGOS

ILLUSTRATION
TANIA RICCI

INTERNATIONAL EDITORIAL DIRECTOR
ANDRÉ L. PASOTTO

EDITORIAL COORDINATOR
RENATA DE SÁ

ENGLISH VERSION
ANA MILITELLO

ART EDITOR
MAURO ROBERTO FERNANDES

Dados Internacionais de Catalogação na Publicação (CIP)
(Câmara Brasileira do Livro, SP, Brasil)

Domingos, Reinaldo
The three penny banks / Reinaldo Domingos ; ilustração Tania Ricci ; tradução Ana Militello. -- 1. ed. -- São Paulo : Editora DSOP, 2020. -- (Explorer ; 1)

Título original: O menino, o dinheiro e os três cofrinhos
ISBN 978-65-87565-16-3

1. Sonhos - Literatura infantojuvenil I. Ricci, Tania. II. Título III. Série.

20-46367 CDD-028.5

Índices para catálogo sistemático:

1. Literatura infantojuvenil 028.5

Aline Graziele Benitez - Bibliotecária - CRB-1/3129

DEAR READER,

MY NAME IS REINALDO, AND JUST LIKE YOU, I WAS ONCE A CHILD. SINCE I WAS LITTLE, I LOVED TO INVENT STORIES AND CREATE IMAGINARY WORLDS. AS I GREW UP, MY BIGGEST DREAM WAS TO SHARE MY STORIES WITH CHILDREN WORLDWIDE.

MY DREAM CAME TRUE. YOU HAVE THE ABILITY TO ACHIEVE YOUR DREAMS TOO. ALL YOU NEED TO DO IS FOLLOW THE FOUR STEPS OF THE METHODOLOGY I CREATED, WHICH YOU WILL LEARN IN THIS BOOK.

BESIDES HELPING YOU TO MAKE YOUR DREAMS COME TRUE, I WANT TO INVITE YOU TO TAKE PART IN THIS STORY WITH ME – BY PAINTING AND DRAWING...

I HOPE YOU ENJOY IT!

ALL THE BEST,

REINALDO DOMINGOS

"EVERY CHILD HAS THE RIGHT TO DREAM,

AND TO MAKE THOSE DREAMS COME TRUE".

Reinaldo Domingos

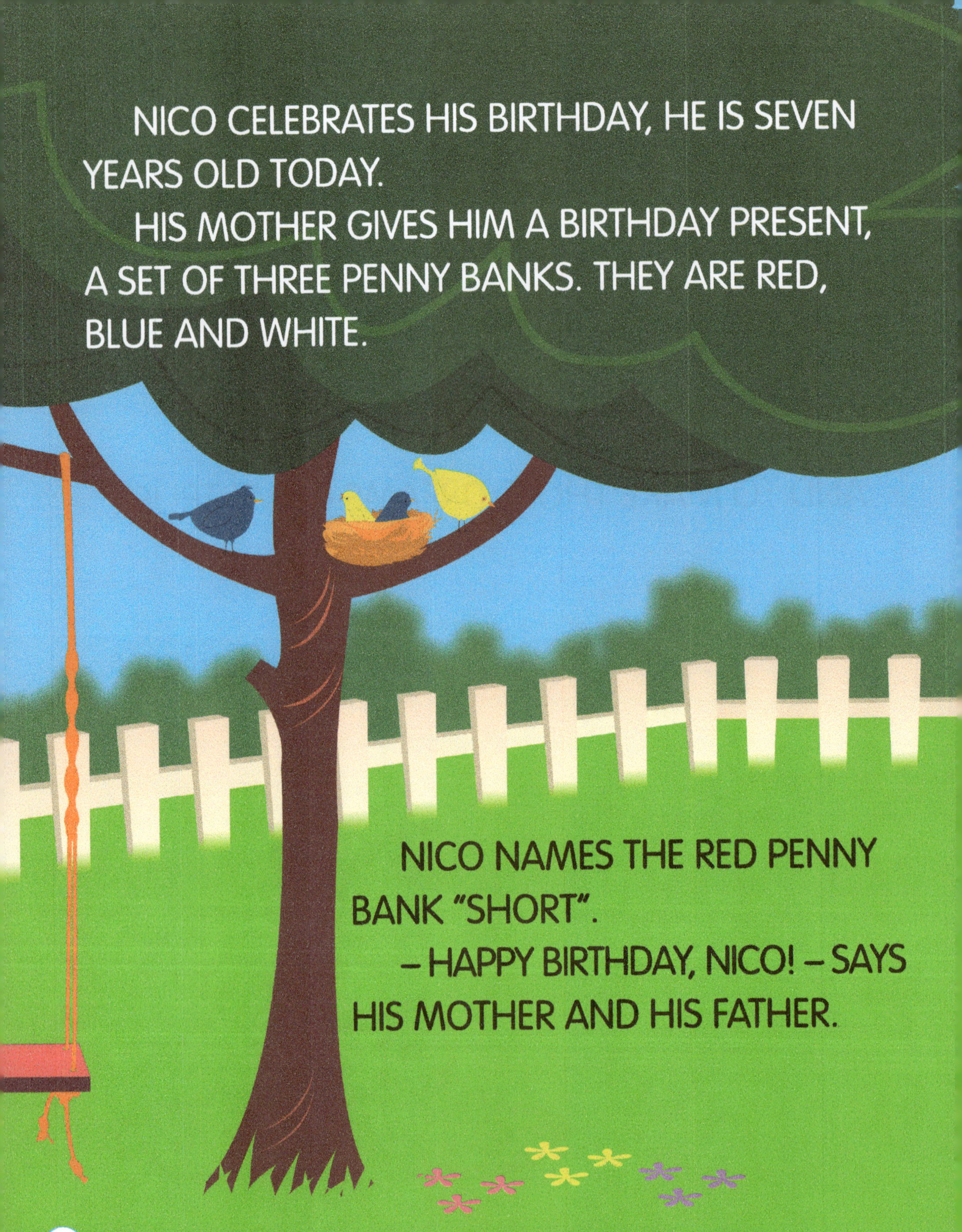

NICO CELEBRATES HIS BIRTHDAY, HE IS SEVEN YEARS OLD TODAY.

HIS MOTHER GIVES HIM A BIRTHDAY PRESENT, A SET OF THREE PENNY BANKS. THEY ARE RED, BLUE AND WHITE.

NICO NAMES THE RED PENNY BANK "SHORT".

– HAPPY BIRTHDAY, NICO! – SAYS HIS MOTHER AND HIS FATHER.

1 CIRCLE.

A) HOW OLD IS NICO?

10 5 7

B) FIND AND CIRCLE NICO'S PRESENT.

____

C) CIRCLE THE NAME OF THE RED PENNY BANK.

SHORT COIN BOY

– HOW CAN A RED PENNY BANK HELP ME?
– CAN IT MAKE MY DREAMS COME TRUE? – ASKS NICO.

– YOU NEED TO SAVE THE COINS YOU GET IN YOUR RED PENNY BANK – SAYS HIS FATHER.

– SOON IT WILL BE FULL.

– THEN YOU CAN OPEN IT, COUNT THE COINS AND USE THEM TO MAKE A DREAM COME TRUE – HIS MOTHER SAYS.

NICO SAVES SOME OF HIS COINS TO MAKE HIS FIRST DREAM COME TRUE: A SOCCER BALL.

– SAVING COINS IS THE SAME AS SAVING BILLS. IT'S IMPORTANT FOR YOU TO LEARN HOW TO SAVE MONEY, SO YOU CAN ACHIEVE YOUR DREAMS – HIS MOTHER SAYS.

2 COUNT AND NUMBER THE BILLS AND THE COINS.

☐ BILLS ☐ COINS

NICO CONTINUES TO SAVE, SAVE, SAVE HIS COINS.

3 CLASS SURVEY. HOW MANY KIDS HAVE A PENNY BANK?

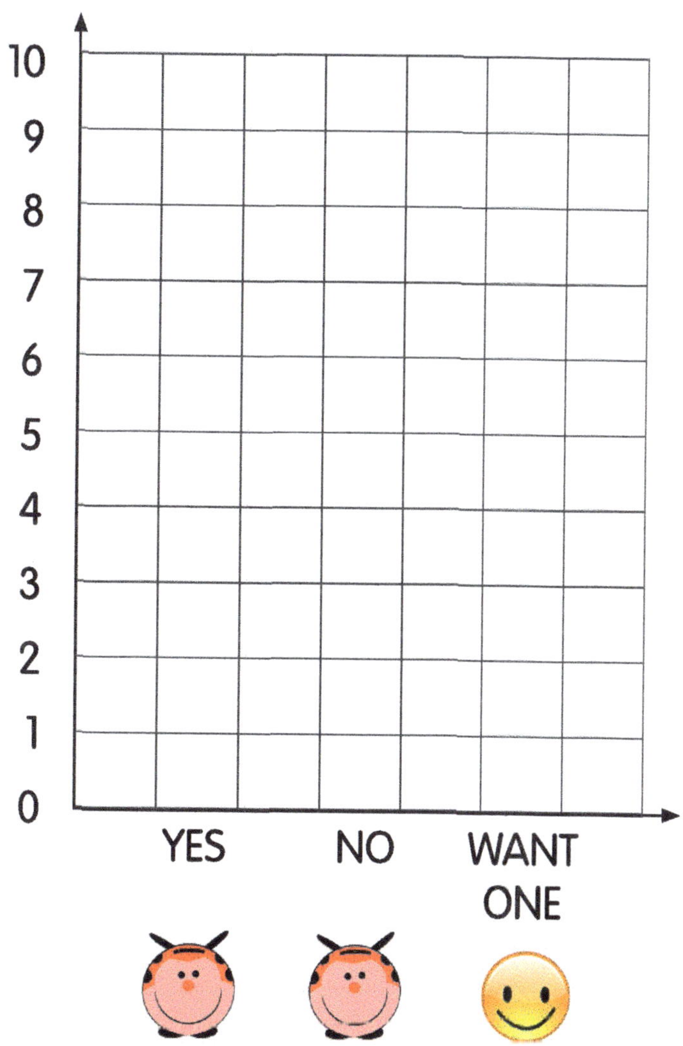

IN A SHORT TIME, THE RED PENNY BANK IS FULL OF COINS.

ONE DAY IT JUST EXPLODED. THE COINS ARE IN THE AIR, LIKE A RAIN OF COINS.

WITH THE COINS FROM THE RED PENNY BANK, NICO DECIDES TO BUY A BAG OF CANDIES, AN ICE CREAM AND MAKE HIS FIRST DREAM COME TRUE, HE BUYS A SOCCER BALL TOO.

4 NUMBER AND COLOR THE PICTURES FOR NICO'S DREAM TO COME TRUE.

THE MOTHER IS SO PROUD OF HER SON AND TELLS HIM TO USE THE BLUE PENNY BANK. NICO HAS A BIGGER DREAM THIS TIME.

THE BLUE PENNY BANK IS BIGGER AND NICO NAMES IT "MEDIUM".

– YOU CAN SAVE MORE COINS TO ACHIEVE YOUR DREAM FASTER. EVERY DREAM TAKES TIME TO COME TRUE – HIS MOTHER EXPLAINS.

NICO STOPS BUYING HIS FAVORITE CANDIES. HE WANTS TO SAVE HIS MONEY TO FILL UP THE BLUE PENNY BANK FASTER.

NICO SAVES, SAVES, AND SAVES HIS COINS.

5 CIRCLE THE SECOND PENNY BANK, MEDIUM.

AFTER SOME TIME IN A BEAUTIFUL DAY, THE BLUE PENNY BANK EXPLODED THE COINS IN THE AIR, LIKE A RAIN OF COINS.

NICO IS HAPPY. IT'S RAINING COINS IN THE AIR.

HE COUNTS ALL THE COINS WITH HIS MOTHER. HIS SECOND DREAM COMES TRUE AND HE BUYS A TOY CAR.

6 DRAW NICO'S SECOND DREAM.

7 WHAT DREAM COSTS MORE? MAKE AN X.

☐ FIRST DREAM

☐ SECOND DREAM

– I'M SO IMPRESSED – SAYS HIS MOTHER WITH A BIG SMILE.

SHE TELLS NICO TO USE THE ENORMOUS WHITE PENNY BANK.

– ITS NAME IS "LONG". IT'S EVEN BIGGER THAN "MEDIUM" AND PLUMPER THAN "SHORT".

NICO KNOWS THE IMPORTANCE OF SAVING AND THAT DREAMS TAKE TIME TO COME TRUE. DREAMS COME TRUE WHEN WE MAKE THE RIGHT CHOICES.

8 FIND AND WRITE THE NAME OF THE WHITE PENNY BANK.

NICO IS HAPPY WITH HIS SOCCER BALL AND TOY CAR. BUT HE UNDERSTANDS THAT TO FEEL REALLY HAPPY, HE NEEDS TO HELP OTHERS, TOO.

NICO WANTS TO HELP HIS FATHER TO MAKE HIS DREAMS COME TRUE.

HE GIVES HIM A PRESENT. IT'S AN ENORMOUS PENNY BANK. NICO'S BIGGEST DREAM IS TO SEE HIS FATHER HAPPY.

9 CIRCLE WHO NICO DECIDES TO HELP TO MAKE A DREAM COME TRUE.

AT FIRST, NICO'S FATHER DOESN'T UNDERSTAND HOW AN ENORMOUS PENNY BANK CAN HELP HIM MAKE HIS DREAMS COME TRUE.

CHOOSE A DREAM AND SAVE ALL THE COINS YOU GET IN THE PENNY BANK – NICO EXPLAINS TO HIS FATHER.

NICO EXPLAINS TO HIS FATHER THAT KEEPING COINS IN THE PENNY BANK IS SAVING. IT'S IMPORTANT TO LEARN HOW TO SAVE TO MAKE DREAMS COME TRUE.

AFTER SOME TIME, YOUR PENNY BANK WILL BE FULL. THEN YOU OPEN IT, COUNT THE COINS AND USE THEM TO MAKE YOUR DREAM COME TRUE – SAYS NICO.

THE FATHER BEGINS TO SAVE ONLY A FEW COINS.

HIS FATHER CONTINUES TO SAVE, SAVE, AND SAVE COINS.

BUT, HIS PENNY BANK DOESN'T EXPLODE COINS IN THE AIR, HE CONTINUES TO SAVE.

NOW, THE FATHER DECIDES TO HELP HIS SON WITH HIS NEW DREAM: TO BUY A BIKE.

IT'S GOING TO TAKE LONGER FOR THIS DREAM TO COME TRUE.

NICO HAS TO SAVE A LOT MORE COINS TO BUY THE BIKE THAN TO BUY A SOCCER BALL OR A TOY CAR.

THE BOY LEARNS THAT IF YOU SAVE MONEY IN THREE PENNY BANKS LIKE SHORT, MEDIUM AND LONG, YOU CAN MAKE MORE DREAMS COME TRUE.

SOME DREAMS HAPPEN IN A SHORTER PERIOD OF TIME. SOME IN A MEDIUM AND SOME CAN TAKE LONGER TO COME TRUE.

HELLO LITTLE FRIEND,

YOU READ THE STORY AND LEARNED THERE ARE SHORT, MEDIUM AND LONG-TERM DREAMS.

DRAW THE DREAMS YOU WANT TO MAKE COME TRUE.

DRAW YOUR SHORT-TERM DREAM. IT CAN BE INDIVIDUAL OR A FAMILY DREAM.

DRAW YOUR MEDIUM-TERM DREAM. IT CAN BE MATERIAL OR NON-MATERIAL.

FINALLY, DRAW THE LONG-TERM DREAM YOU AND YOUR FAMILY WANT TO COME TRUE.

A VERY SPECIAL MESSAGE FROM DSOP

To the teachers or parents/ guardians

Congratulations, you just took the first step towards an investment with an invaluable return: prosperity, in every moment of your family's life, beginning with your young student!

The **DSOP Methodology** illustrates how important it is to have dreams in our lives, and above all how to achieve them. It focuses upon behavioural development, with the goal of creating a healthier financial life. This makes it possible to build a life filled with accomplishments.

The DSOP books, courses and educational programmes for children and young people also include content which extends to family members and school staff. The guidance given, both in the manuals and projects offered to teachers and from the DSOP advisors and pedagogical support team, will help your young student to transform their life, inspired by the captivating and entrepreneurial paths taken by the characters in the stories.

There is growing awareness internationally of the importance of incorporating Financial Education in school curriculums. In some cases, this is combined with teaching students to develop conscious behaviour around consumption practices. The UN proposed the 17 Sustainable Development Goals (SNGs) and included **Responsible**

MENSAGEM MUITO ESPECIAL DA DSOP

Aos responsáveis pelos alunos ou seus familiares

Parabéns, você acaba de dar o primeiro passo rumo a um investimento de retorno inestimável: a prosperidade em todos os momentos da vida da sua família, começando pelo jovem estudante da sua casa!

A **Metodologia DSOP** mostra a importância dos sonhos em nossas vidas e, especialmente, como alcançá-los. O foco está no desenvolvimento comportamental para uma vida financeira mais saudável. Assim, é possível construir uma vida cheia de realizações.

Os livros, cursos e programas educacionais para crianças e jovens também são complementados por conteúdos que se estendem à sua família e funcionários da escola. Com o apoio das orientações dos manuais e projetos oferecidos aos professores e da assessoria e suporte pedagógicos da DSOP, eles ajudarão o jovem estudante a transformar a vida inspirado nas adoráveis trajetórias empreendedoras das personagens.

A BNCC (Base Nacional Comum Curricular) tornou obrigatório nas escolas públicas e privadas o ensino de Educação Financeira nos Anos Iniciais e Finais do Ensino Fundamental, porém voltado para que os alunos desenvolvam um comportamento de consumo consciente. A própria ONU propõe os 17 Objetivos de Sustentabilidade

MENSAJE MUY ESPECIAL DE DSOP

A las familias de los alumnos o sus responsables

¡Felicitaciones! Usted acaba de dar el primer paso rumbo a una inversión de valor inestimable: la prosperidad en todos los momentos de la vida de su familia, empezando por los jóvenes estudiantes de su casa.

La **Metodología DSOP** potencia la valoración de los sueños en nuestras vidas y, especialmente, cómo alcanzarlos. El énfasis está en el desarrollo comportamental hacia una vida financiera más saludable, pues así es posible construir una vida de realizaciones. Los libros, cursos y programas educacionales para jóvenes son también complementados por contenidos que alcanzan a sus familias y toda la comunidad escolar.

Con el apoyo de las orientaciones de los manuales, proyectos, asesoría y soporte pedagógicos de la Editorial DSOP, los profesores ayudarán a su joven estudiante a transformar su vida, inspirado en las adorables trayectorias emprendedoras de los personajes.

En Brasil hay leyes que han vuelto obligatoria en las escuelas públicas y privadas la enseñanza de la Educación Financiera volcada hacia el desarrollo de un comportamiento de consumo consciente. La misma ONU propone 17 Objetivos de Sustentabilidad para la Humanidad e incluye **Consumption**, refiriéndose exactamente a esa cuestión.

Consumption, referring to precisely this objective.

For over 10 years, Reinaldo Domingos PhD has been sharing his methodology with the world via the DSOP group. It has brought great success not only for him, but also for all the Financial Educators and Financial Therapists who have graduated during this decade, as well as, more recently, through franchises. Its efficiency has been proven not only in practice, but also by the academic and scientific world; his methodology has been championed in the United States at universally commended master, doctoral and post-doctoral levels.

When it comes to behaviour, the best way to develop it swiftly and achieve efficient results is to start as early as possible and maintain consistency. We need to begin preparing ourselves for adult life in childhood, and by doing so we can achieve financial independence earlier than previous generations, and dedicate our efforts and time towards realising our own dreams and those of the people we love.

So, how does this transformational methodology work? Learn more and win a free e-book on *DSOP Financial Education Methodology*, visit the link or QR Code on the back cover of this book.

para a Humanidade e incluiu o **Consumption**, referindo-se exatamente a esse objetivo.

Há mais de 10 anos, por meio do Grupo DSOP, o PhD Reinaldo Domingos tem compartilhado com o mundo sua metodologia vivenciada com sucesso não só por ele, como também por todos os Educadores Financeiros e Terapeutas Financeiros formados ao longo dessa década, além do trabalho mais recente com os franqueados. Não só a prática comprovou sua eficiência, mas também o mundo acadêmico e científico, pois sua metodologia também foi defendida nos Estados Unidos em níveis de mestrado, doutorado e pós-doutorado aprovados com louvor e de forma unânime.

Quando falamos de comportamento, a melhor maneira de desenvolvê-lo rapidamente rumo aos resultados eficientes, é começando o quanto antes e mantendo a continuidade. Desde criança, temos que nos preparar para a vida adulta; assim, poderemos nos tornar independentes mais cedo que as gerações anteriores e direcionar nossos esforços e tempo, a partir de então, para a realização de sonhos próprios e os de quem amamos.

Mas, como é essa metodologia transformadora? Saiba mais e ganhe um e-book sobre a *Metodologia DSOP de Educação Financeira*, por meio do QR Code atrás deste livro.

Hace más de 10 años, por medio del Grupo DSOP, el PhD Reinaldo Domingos ha compartido su metodología vivenciada con éxito no solo por él sino por todos los Educadores Financieros y Terapeutas financieros formados en sus cursos. Además de toda la comprobación práctica, está también el reconocimiento académico y científico, pues la Metodología DSOP ha sido defendida en los EEUU en niveles de máster, de doctorado y posdoctorado.

Cuando se trata de comportamiento, para garantizar resultados eficientes en el futuro, lo mejor es desarrollarlo lo más pronto posible, además de mantener su continuidad. Desde niños, debemos ir preparándonos para los principales retos de la vida adulta, para volvernos independientes financieramente aún antes de la edad en la que las generaciones anteriores lo lograban. Así, podremos concentrarnos a partir de entonces no solo en disfrutar de los sueños ya alcanzados, sino también a multiplicarlos e incluir a quienes amamos en esa trayectoria.

Pero, ¿cómo es esa metodología transformadora? Para saberlo, infórmese mejor y adquiera su e-book sobre Educación Financiera en el código QR detrás de este libro.

REINALDO DOMINGOS WAS BORN IN CASA BRANCA, A SMALL TOWN IN THE STATE OF SÃO PAULO, BRAZIL. HIS FATHER WAS A RAILWAY WORKER AND HIS MOTHER A SELF-EMPLOYED WORKER. AT THE AGE OF 12, HE DREAMED OF HAVING A BIKE. HE CREATED A METHOD OF SAVING SOME MONEY EVERY MONTH TO MAKE HIS DREAM COME TRUE. THIS METHOD BECAME THE BASIS OF THE DSOP METHODOLOGY: A SIMPLE AND EFFICIENT WAY OF MANAGING MONEY, CHANGING CONSUMPTION HABITS AND MAKING DREAMS COME TRUE.